Science Biographies

Louis
Pasteur

Nick Hunter

Raintree is an imprint of Capstone Global Library Limited, a company incorporated in England and Wales having its registered office at 7 Pilgrim Street, London, EC4V 6LB – Registered company number: 6695582

www.raintreepublishers.co.uk
myorders@raintreepublishers.co.uk

Edited by Dan Nunn, Adam Miller, and Diyan Leake
Designed by Cynthia Akiyoshi
Original illustrations © Capstone Global Library Ltd 2014
Illustrated by Cynthia Akiyoshi
Picture research by Hannah Taylor and Tracy Cummins
Production by Helen McCreath
Originated by Capstone Global Library
Printed and bound in China

ISBN 978 1 406 27241 3
17 16 15 14 13
10 9 8 7 6 5 4 3 2 1

Hunter, Nick
Pasteur, Louis. (Science Biographies)
A full catalogue record for this book is available from the British Library.

Acknowledgements
We would like to thank the following for permission to reproduce photographs: Alamy p. 28 (© The Print Collector); The Bridgeman Art Library p. 6 left and right (Pasteur, Louis (1822–95); Musee Pasteur, Institut Pasteur, Paris, France; Archives Charmet); Corbis pp. 5 (Tarker), 13 (Simko/Visuals Unlimited, Inc.), 15 (Bettmann), 22 (Stefano Bianchetti); Getty Images pp. 8 (Roger Viollet Collection), 9 (Time Life Pictures/Mansell), 10 (Hulton Archive), 12 (Prisma/UIG), 17 (Rue des Archives/PVDE), 19 (Apic), 20 (Rischgitz), 21 (Issouf Sanogo/AFP), 25 (Universal History Archive), 27 (Hulton Archive); Institut Pasteur p. 18; Shutterstock p. 16 (© fotohunter), design elements (© Zerbor, © Sebastian Kaulitzki, © titelio, © Luisa Fumi, © Anna Kucherova, © Victoria Kalinina, © Dennis Tokarzewski); Superstock pp. 4 (The Art Archive), 11 (The Art Archive), 23 (The Art Archive), 24 (CDC), 26 (Pixtal).

Cover photograph of Louis Pasteur reproduced with permission of Photo Researchers (SPL/Science Source) and *Eschericia coli* bacteria reproduced with permission of Getty Images (Dr David Phillips).

Contents

Some words are shown in **bold**, like this. You can find out what they mean by looking in the glossary.

Who was Louis Pasteur?

Louis Pasteur spent his life trying to understand the world of **microbes**. Microbes can only be seen under a **microscope**, but they are everywhere around us. They cause diseases, but they also help humans and animals in many ways. Louis Pasteur studied and experimented with microbes. He explained more about how they work than any other scientist. His discoveries saved millions of lives.

Louis Pasteur's discoveries made him famous around the world.

When Pasteur was born, scientists understood little about the tiny living things they could see through microscopes. Pasteur was able to prove that microbes caused many natural processes, such as turning milk sour. He was also able to explain where these germs came from and how they caused diseases.

New ideas

Pasteur's discoveries made him famous. They also challenged what other scientists believed. Scientists and other people often disagreed with Pasteur's ideas, but he was able to prove them wrong.

Pasteur worked long hours in his **laboratory** to solve the mysteries of microscopic life.

Family

Louis Pasteur was born in Dole, a town in eastern France, on 27 December 1822. His father was a tanner, who made animal skins into leather. Louis later said that his father had taught him the importance of hard work.

Louis was a talented artist and painted these pictures of his parents.

A proud Frenchman

When Louis was born in 1822, France was just recovering from many years of **revolution** and war. The war had ended when French emperor Napoleon was defeated by Britain and other European countries at the Battle of Waterloo in 1815. Louis' father had fought in the war, and Louis was always a proud Frenchman.

While Louis was still young, the family moved to nearby Arbois. Louis went to the local primary school. He did not do well at school but studied hard. His hard work paid off at secondary school. One of his teachers told his father that Louis had a chance of training as a teacher at France's best teaching college. Louis passed his **degree** in science in the college at nearby Besançon and headed to France's capital, Paris.

Paris was a long way from home for the young scientist.

Learning and teaching

When Pasteur started working in the laboratory at the École Normale Supérieure in Paris, he knew that he had found his life's work. He worked with some of France's greatest scientists. He became a doctor of science in 1847. However, at the time, there were not many chances to work in scientific research.

Pasteur's parents were worried that their son would be distracted from his studies by the social whirl of Paris, but he was dedicated to his work.

Pasteur left Paris in 1848 to teach science at a school in Dijon, but he really wanted to spend his time in the laboratory. He soon accepted a job as Professor of Chemistry at the University of Strasbourg.

MARRYING MARIE

In 1849, Pasteur married Marie Laurent, whose father was head of the university. In 1854, the couple moved to the city of Lille, where Pasteur was offered a better job at the city's university.

Ambition

Shortly after arriving in Strasbourg, Pasteur wrote to Marie's father asking if he could marry her. His letter included details of his family. It also said that he planned to become a member of the Academy of Sciences, a society made up of France's very best scientists.

This portrait shows the young Pasteur around the time of his marriage to Marie.

Solving problems

The Pasteurs' new home city was at the centre of French **industry**. Pasteur used his knowledge of science to solve the problems of local businesses. A local brewer complained to Pasteur that his business was losing money because the beer he made was turning sour. Studying the beer under a microscope, Pasteur could see tiny living things, or microbes.

Pasteur carried out detailed experiments on the contents of these **vats** to understand what happened to the beer.

Pasteur also looked at other substances that turned sour, including milk and wine. He worked out that microbes called **bacteria** caused the sourness. He also discovered that these bacteria played an important part in making beer and wine.

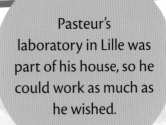

Fermentation

People had produced wine and beer by the process of **fermentation** for thousands of years before Pasteur was able to explain the process. Fermentation is a change caused by microbes. There are many examples in what we eat and drink, including the souring of milk or using **yeast** to make bread.

Pasteur's laboratory in Lille was part of his house, so he could work as much as he wished.

Pasteurization in Paris

By 1857, Pasteur heard about a job at his old college in Paris. He moved his family to France's capital. His fame grew when he wrote and gave lectures about his ideas on fermentation.

Pasteur's explanations and help for French industry brought him to the attention of Emperor Napoleon III. Making wine was big business, but there was a problem. Wine also turned sour, and this meant that French wine producers could not ship it to other countries.

Whining about wine

Pasteur's work on wine also helped the French navy. Sailors were unhappy with the sour-tasting wine they had to drink at sea. Navy officials were worried that the sailors would **mutiny** because of this.

Heat treatment

Pasteur discovered that by heating wine he could kill the microbe that spoiled the wine. This saved the French wine industry. It also worked with other substances. Next time you pour milk on your breakfast cereal, look at the carton. You will find that the milk is pasteurized. This means it has been heated to kill microbes. This is the process that Louis Pasteur developed.

This is what the microbes in milk look like under a microscope.

Where do microbes come from?

Scientists at the time believed that microbes could appear out of nothing as chemicals changed. Pasteur was sure that microbes came into substances such as milk from outside. In 1859, he set out to prove he was right.

PROVING HIS POINT

Pasteur boiled some beef **broth** in a flask with a long, thin neck. Microbes from the air were trapped in the neck and did not reach the broth, so it stayed clear. When Pasteur broke off the neck of the flask, the broth soon went cloudy. This proved that microbes came from the air.

Pasteur's experiment was very simple. He carefully planned it to prove his ideas about microbes.

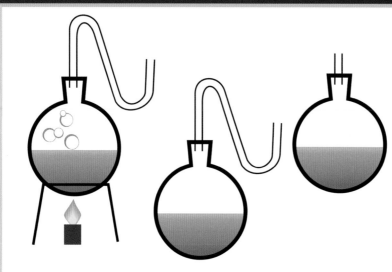

| Broth is boiled | Broth remains free of micro-organisms | Curved neck is removed | Micro-organisms grow in broth |

Joseph Lister (1827–1912)

Joseph Lister was a well-known **surgeon** in Glasgow, Scotland, when he read Pasteur's ideas about microbes. He discovered that if he cleaned his patients' wounds and the instruments he used, there was much less chance of wounds being **infected**.

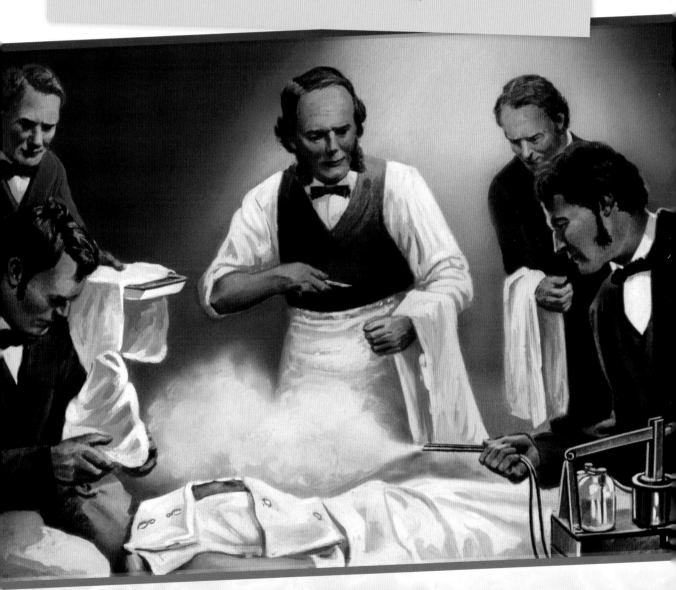

Save the silkworm

Pasteur was now a respected scientist. In 1862, he became a member of the Academy of Sciences. When the **silkworms** that were essential for the French silk industry started dying from a mysterious disease, there was only one man to call.

Silkworms are not worms – they are caterpillars! They spin cocoons when they become moths. People use these cocoons to make silk.

In 1865, Pasteur travelled to the south of France to investigate. His research lasted five years.

He worked with a team of assistants and was even helped by his wife. Together, they studied the silkworms and found that there were two different diseases affecting them. Eventually, Pasteur found a way to stop the diseases from spreading, but he could not cure them. He discovered that dealing with diseases was much more complex than his previous work.

Marie Pasteur helped her husband with his work on silkworms.

Too strict for his students

Pasteur was a great scientist, but he did not impress everyone. In 1867, he was forced to leave the École Normale in Paris after students complained about his strict discipline. Pasteur became a professor at the Sorbonne, France's most famous college. He was not put in charge of student discipline there.

Personal tragedy

While each new triumph made Pasteur more famous in the science community, his home life was much more troubled.

The Pasteurs had five children. Between 1859 and 1866, three of their four daughters died from illness. These tragedies may have pushed Pasteur to devote himself to curing diseases.

Searching for truth

"Happiness now exists only in searching for truth in one of its many forms," Pasteur wrote to a colleague after the deaths of his daughters.

This photo shows three of Pasteur's children: Jean-Baptiste (left), Cécile (middle), and Marie-Louise (right).

Illness and war

In 1868, Pasteur himself was forced to cut down his huge workload when he became ill. He suffered a **stroke** and could not move one side of his body. His work was also interrupted when war broke out between France and the German state of Prussia in 1871, forcing the family to leave Paris.

A rare failure

Pasteur's work was not always a triumph. In 1865, he tried to find the cause of a disease called **cholera**, which had broken out in the city of Marseilles. He failed, but this spurred him on to find out more about how microbes cause disease in humans.

Marie Pasteur supported her husband's work and managed their household.

Infectious disease

Pasteur returned to Paris when the war ended in 1871. For the rest of his life, Pasteur tackled the problems of human and animal diseases.

In 1871, doctors believed that diseases developed on their own inside the body, or were caused by bad air and unhealthy conditions. Pasteur knew that his work on microbes held the key to understanding disease. He believed that microbes, or germs, attacked the body from outside.

By the 1870s, Pasteur was too ill to teach students. The French government paid him to continue his research.

Anthrax is a deadly disease that killed many sheep and people in the 1800s. Pasteur found the microbe that caused the disease and set to work trying to cure it.

What is vaccination?

A **vaccine** infects a person with a small quantity of the microbes that cause a particular disease. It enables the body's **immune system** to fight the disease so that the person will not catch it. Pasteur's understanding of the cause of disease enabled him to build on the work done by English doctor Edward Jenner and Asian doctors who had developed early vaccines.

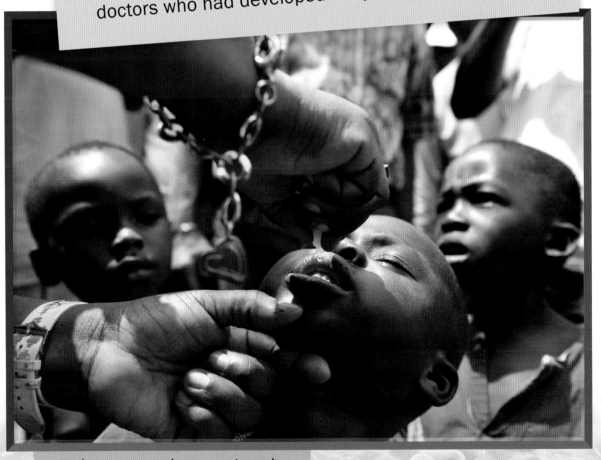

Today, most people are vaccinated against diseases.

A challenge

Pasteur had been mocked and attacked for his idea that germs caused diseases. It went against the ideas of most scientists. Pasteur was quick to accept a challenge in 1881, when a vet claimed Pasteur's vaccine for anthrax would not work.

At the vet's farm in Pouilly-le-Fort, near Paris, Pasteur arranged a public experiment using 70 animals. Half the animals were vaccinated against anthrax and the other half were not. When they were all injected with the disease, only the vaccinated animals survived. Pasteur had proved his point.

Pasteur's experiment attracted huge interest. Politicians, writers, and farmers came to see the vaccine test.

Rivals in science

Pasteur was always careful to **publish** his ideas only when he was sure he had the answer. He did not want to give his **rivals** any clues about his work. His biggest rival was the German scientist Robert Koch. Koch also believed that germs caused disease, but the two men often criticized each other's work.

Robert Koch and Pasteur never worked together, but they are both remembered for the discovery of the germ theory of disease.

The battle against rabies

Pasteur now tried to find a vaccine for rabies.
This horrible disease is usually caught by
a bite from an infected animal. As always,
Pasteur put huge effort into his new project,
hardly leaving time to eat and sleep.

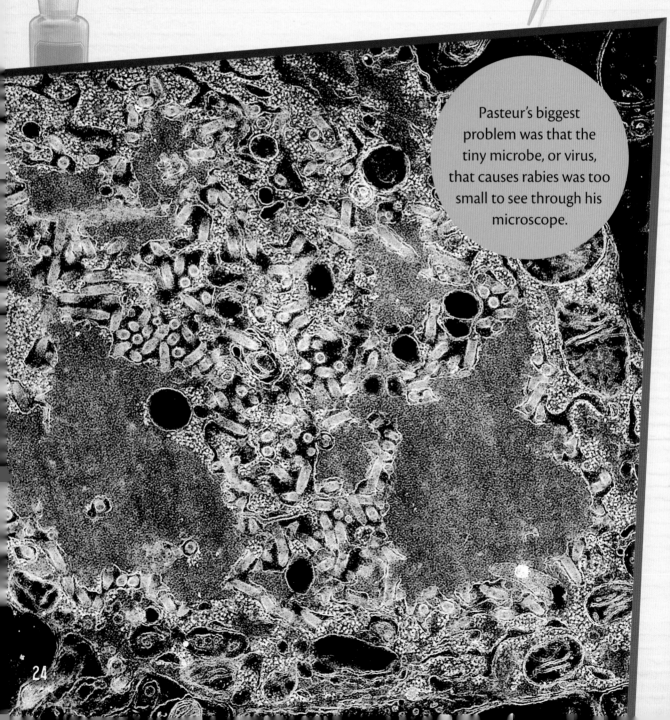

Pasteur's biggest problem was that the tiny microbe, or virus, that causes rabies was too small to see through his microscope.

24

Pasteur used animals in his experiments to find out how the rabies **virus** behaved. He needed to see what happened when a human caught rabies, but he was not allowed to experiment on people. Pasteur even considered injecting himself with rabies to test the vaccine he had created.

Animal welfare

As they tried to understand deadly diseases, Pasteur and other scientists infected and killed many animals. Many people opposed these experiments. Scientists argued that their work would save many more human and animal lives in the future. Debates about the use of animals in science experiments continue today.

Joseph Meister had been bitten by a dog with rabies. Pasteur's treatment stopped him from getting the disease.

JOSEPH MEISTER

In October 1885, Pasteur announced that his vaccine for rabies had been used on nine-year-old Joseph Meister. The treatment was a success, and requests for a vaccine started to pour in from around the world.

Final years

His work on rabies meant that Pasteur's fame spread far beyond the scientific world. He was recognized as his country's greatest ever scientist. In 1881, Pasteur became a member of the Académie Française, an exclusive society made up of 40 of France's most important people.

Pasteur was not alone in his work on rabies and other diseases. A team of researchers worked with him. Pasteur's work on disease would have been less successful without them.

By the time of his death, Pasteur was a national hero in France.

CONTINUING HIS WORK

In 1887, work began on the Pasteur Institute, which would continue Pasteur's research long after his death. It was opened in 1888 and became Pasteur's home and laboratory. By this time, his health was fading. Pasteur died on 28 September 1895.

Pasteur continued to work in his laboratory for as long as his health allowed.

Following Pasteur

Pasteur would be amazed by the advances in medicine since his death. Many diseases have been cured and scientists using the latest technology know much more about how diseases grow and spread. Without the work of Louis Pasteur and others who first explored the world of microbes, none of this would have been possible.

In search of Pasteur

Almost every town in France has a street, a school, or a library named after Louis Pasteur, and there are many ways we can find out about his life. The rooms he worked in have been kept as a museum at the Pasteur Institute in Paris, where visitors can see the equipment he used. Pasteur's laboratory notebooks have also been kept. They show that he made many more mistakes and failed experiments than Pasteur revealed in his lifetime.

Newspapers at the time reported on Pasteur's greatest discoveries.

Le Petit Journal

Le Petit Journal
CHAQUE JOUR 5 CENTIMES
Le Supplément Illustré
CHAQUE SEMAINE 5 CENTIMES

SUPPLÉMENT ILLUSTRÉ
Huit pages : CINQ centimes

ABONNEMENTS

Sixième année

DIMANCHE 13 OCTOBRE 1895

Numéro 256

A LOUIS PASTEUR

Timeline

1822 Louis Pasteur is born in Dole, France, on 27 December

1842 Earns a science degree from a college in nearby Besançon

1843 Begins studying at École Normale Supérieure in Paris, where he learns from some of France's most important scientists

1849 Starts work as professor of chemistry at the University of Strasbourg; marries Marie Laurent

1854 Starts working at the university in Lille, where he first studies the role of microbes in fermentation

1857 Moves to Paris where his work on fermentation continues

1859 The Pasteurs' eldest daughter Jeanne dies from the disease typhoid

1862 Pasteur becomes a member of the Academy of Sciences

1865 Begins work on problems of disease in silkworms. Daughter Camille dies

1866 Daughter Cécile dies

1867 Pasteur loses his job at École Normale Supérieure; becomes professor at the Sorbonne

1877 Begins to study infectious diseases in animals and humans

1881 Carries out public demonstration of anthrax vaccine at Pouilly-le-Fort; becomes member of Académie Française

1885 Carries out successful treatment of Joseph Meister with a rabies vaccine

1895 Louis Pasteur dies on 28 September

Glossary

bacterium (plural: **bacteria**) type of microbe that lives in soil, water, or the bodies of living things. Some bacteria cause disease but others are important for many natural processes.

broth liquid in which meat or vegetables have been cooked

cholera deadly disease that can affect the digestive systems of humans and other animals

degree qualification given by a university or college

fermentation chemical reaction in which substances are broken down and energy is released. Fermentation is part of the production of many foods, including bread and wine.

immune system body system that protects the body from disease

industry business that produces products to sell, often in large factories

infected to be attacked by a microbe that causes disease, such as when a wound is infected with bacteria

laboratory place where science experiments and research are carried out

microbe any tiny living thing that can only be seen with a microscope, including bacteria and viruses

microscope instrument through which objects are magnified so they appear much bigger, so scientists can examine tiny objects such as microbes

mutiny uprising or rebellion, particularly on board a ship

publish make information or ideas available to people, such as in a printed book

revolution sudden change of government, often because of a violent rebellion

rival one of two people trying to reach the same goal

silkworm type of caterpillar, which spins a cocoon that is used to make silk thread

stroke damage to the brain caused by lack of blood flow, which can lead to problems with movement and speech

surgeon doctor who performs operations on patients

vaccine small amount of a disease that is used to prevent a patient catching the disease

vat large tub used to hold liquids

virus tiny microbe that can cause disease

yeast type of microbe that causes fermentation and is used in baking bread and making alcoholic drinks

Find out more

Books

Epidemics and Plagues, Richard Walker (Kingfisher, 2009)

Louis Pasteur (Great Scientists: Levelled Biographies), Liz Miles
(Raintree, 2009)

Louis Pasteur and Pasteurization (Graphic Inventions and Discoveries),
Jennifer Fandel (Raintree, 2011)

Micro-organisms (Super Science), Rob Colson (Franklin Watts, 2013)

Websites

**www.bbc.co.uk/schools/scienceclips/ages/10_11/micro_organisms.
shtml**
Test your knowledge of microbes with this game and quiz.

www.sciencekids.co.nz/sciencefacts/scientists/louispasteur.html
Find a biography of Louis Pasteur and other fun features on this website.

www.sciencemuseum.org.uk/broughttolife/people/louispasteur.aspx
This biography of Louis Pasteur from the Science Museum includes links
to related topics.

Place to visit

Wellcome Collection
183 Euston Road
London NW1 2BE
Tel.: 0207 611 2222
www.wellcomecollection.org
This centre is set up to explore the connections between medicine,
life, and art in the past, present, and future. A Young Explorer's Pack is
provided for visitors aged 5–10 years.

Index